EATING IN THE UNDERWORLD

EATING IN THE

WESLEYAN POETRY

UNDERWORLD

RACHEL ZUCKER

WESLEYAN UNIVERSITY PRESS

MIDDLETOWN, CONNECTICUT

PUBLISHED BY WESLEYAN UNIVERSITY PRESS

MIDDLETOWN, CT 06459

© 2003 BY RACHEL ZUCKER

ALL RIGHTS RESERVED

PRINTED IN THE UNITED STATES OF AMERICA

LIBRARY OF CONGRESS CATALOGING-IN-PUBLICATION DATA

ZUCKER, RACHEL

EATING IN THE UNDERWORLD / RACHEL ZUCKER.

P. CM. — (WESLEYAN POETRY)

ISBN 0-8195-6627-6 (CLOTH : ALK. PAPER) —

ISBN 0-8195-6628-4 (PBK. : ALK. PAPER)

I. TITLE. II. SERIES.

PS3626.U26 E25 2003

811'.6—DC21 2002152722

Grateful acknowledgment is made to the editors of the following publications in which these poems or versions of these poems first appeared: *3rd Bed, Colorado Review, Columbia Journal, Epoch, Explosive Magazine, Fourteen Hills, New Letters, Pleiades, Prairie Schooner,* and *Volt.*

Thank you to Larry Sandomir, John Aune, Wayne Koestenbaum, Nancy Kricorian, Lois Conner, David Trinidad, Phyllis Rosen, Jorie Graham, and Brenda Hillman for guidance and inspiration, and to these kind and careful readers: Brian Cassidy, Ben Mosher, Katy Lederer, John O'Connor, Kevin Prufer, Wylie O'Sullivan, Tom Shakow, and Arielle Greenberg. Thanks to Joan, Josh, and most of all to Doug Powell.

Excerpt from "Wuthering Heights" from *Crossing the Water* by Sylvia Plath. Copyright © 1962 by Ted Hughes. Reprinted by permission of HarperCollins Publishers Inc.

for my mother who wrote down my dreams

for my father and his faith

and for Josh

Contents

[ONE]

here there is no place

that does not see you . . .

RAINER MARIA RILKE

If the light were good I could see everything.
Look through rain, live the even life.

I, who have been pressed and prettied,
feel more watched than wandering,

wonder, does someone expect me?
Today wind, like water pulling back

the pebble-layer, wants to sigh, the big stones
heave and settle. But before the ribs expand

it pulls again.
I crave—

but damn these maidens won't allow . . .
The light is just a likeness,

      (if I could only show them—)

oh what does the wind want?

a light as if pure and white were one word:
scrito, stepping twice

am I real alone? alone, alone
what waves are for

I cannot afford this sky
or the sky to move on

watching the dead go in, the tides come out
the light might not be the same again

all the light turns green at once
go go go go go

I will
go, not even knowing

where

it seems so simple
this sea

my voice carries (flag snapping, crack of static)
and comes back to me:

> *no one dies in the land of the dead*

Not even the moon saw me withdraw.

I grasped my chastity and swallowed it
into the lower crescent of my belly.

What is it good for? Where does it take me?
Only on cool nights will I need its light

to show me the way toward passion.

The dead draw blood from my shadow
as I walk among them.

I realize now
it was the foreground

that opened up,
not the ground.

There was a seam in that sulphurous
strand and though afraid of water,

I stepped in. Away from where the body
of my mother is everywhere.

DIARY [UNDERWORLD]

My toes reflected in the bath water make a shape.

    When I wiggle the big one, two move.

I am still alive.

Hot body in hot bath, the cool stream jets invisibly underwater.
    Spout submerged scalding raw, wrinkled fingers.
    Cool moving through hot, around hot, pockets
    of little atmospheres.
    The only thing left to feel:
the mix of fevers.

    Remember the beginning, before science was necessary?

Now we know hot does not change cold in any way.
    They move around each other:
    spreading each other out—first pockets, then harder to recognize—
    spreading each other apart, still cold and hot, broken into pieces:
molecules.

Anyone could mistake it for tepid,
    that which is scalding and frozen at once.

Somewhere between a father and lover
but not *my* father or any lover possible.

He says *to say 'the heat hit like a wave' is not to account
for this impeccable stillness.*

He says when I turn my head away it's like the word *broken*.

And I am not the same when I look back
to where the world and its thick air are examples:

moth in a glass walkway; he calls me *lambent*, *lucent*.

I have changed form, but such things don't matter.
It's so hot the thin-skinned lemons are weeping.

Isn't this what I wanted? Sick of deciduous life,
the dappled light, pointillist neighborhoods—

He leads me where no one has invented comfort.

He says *July is a perfect month for snowfall.*

LETTER [DEMETER TO PERSEPHONE]

In your place

    there was

       a dry color

           turmeric?

        cinnamon, cumin, cayenne?

but not like color, more like
    cloves, cardamom, coriander

            like coarse-cut salt on the tongue—

      if I taste it will I know?

what is the color of fish in the river Styx?

        Thumbprints and tracks
        inside the door, lights left on
        in the room, small things lying about—

    days and days and days you have been gone

At home, the bells were a high light-yellow
with no silver or gray just buttercup or sugar-and-lemon.

Here bodies are lined in blue against the sea.
And where red is red there is only red.

I have to be blue to bathe in the sea.
Red, to live in the red room with red air

to rest my head, red cheek down, on the red table.

Above, it was so green: brown, yellow, white, green.
My longing for red furious, sexual.

There things were alive but nothing moved.
Now I live near the sea in a place which has no blue and is not the sea.

Gulls flock, leeward then tangent
and pigeons bully them off the ground.

Hardly alive, almost blind—a hot geometry casts off
every color of the world. Everything moves, nothing alive.

In the red room there is a sky which is painted over in red
but is not red and was, once, the sky.

This is how I live.

A red table in a red room filled with red air.
A woman, edged in blue, bathing in the blue sea.

The surface like the pale, scaled skin of fish
far below or above or away—

many cities no longer exist
but there is cleaning to finish

lemon halves wrapped
in clinging plastic

arms invisible around me
the only sun

lightning

the night a chance
to be ready for morning

Even my handwriting is lonely.
Severed legs and spinnerets,

abandoned dolmens—
Tonight a wind without direction

    (echo without origin)
confess, unsettles . . .

I spread oil over my shoulders
knowing you watch me.

I don't remember killing these spiders
or wanting your name.

The hand pulls up through water,
trails of resistance follow

like bridal trains, exhausted
smoothed-out ripples,

and rests palm-up on the surface.
Buoyant and lifeless, open.

The body would make this shape
if it knew how.

If the body could bend.
If the mind would let it,

cupped but not hollow.

We would not feel our own flying
and would move faster than anyone
could track our progress.

If one senses motion at all it is falling,
but this is a misperception:
we would be falling upward.

Like the sound of ocean
if you live life as a fish.
Loosen your photographs from the walls
but leave them hanging.

He gives me the wedding band of the real world
a story with pockets and mirrors

woos me with music that could kill insects
its frequency

reveals men in the distance forging the bridge
between nether and either

when night sets, the stones return to the earth

and in the morning, work again:
swimming through chaos to find the world

You will find ardor.

Congeal, extract, distill—
one thousand times.
Solid to vapor and vapor to solid;
you move too quickly for rain.

Sublimed, we are changed
—elixir, transmute, refined—
face and chest scrape
below the surf: afferent polestars
invert, invert.

The flagstone trail winds serpentine through
he loves me and he loves me

thrum of prayer behind talk
sky a background of birds

the ache and savor
of flowers out of season

NOTE [HADES TO PERSEPHONE]

Spin to breathe.
Only the still world passing
as you flee reminds you to
fill and empty lungs
when you have forgotten
how to blink.

Would that I were not an only child,
that she'd find other models to subject to her affections

here silk and paper flowers
a landscape, no horizon—

and it isn't the sky that matters
but if I fly through

the frame, a window, distributes time
across dimensions: I would not stop it if I could

NOTE [HADES TO PERSEPHONE]

All over the world women
are dreaming
of the same child.
Fingers poised
around a golden tiger's-eye.

I fear that she will find you,
that there is a chemical
she might trace to reveal
your many paths.

It is hard enough to go down, but to bring back up—
like trying to fill the ocean

down is fast, full of infinity of event
a bush burning and burning but

we do not run out of words or
space around the figure

the one-liner
ocean liner

my love is a collector who
keeps his butterflies alive

NOTE [HADES TO PERSEPHONE]

No choice but to scratch words
sworn unutterable.
I rush to hold you:
a salamander.

I break lines, pulverize parchment
swallow God's name

enter the inverted ziggurat but cannot
hide in architecture

my hands are pinned to pages
not a set, but still matching

If she could trust enough
to stop and see
your crisscrossed wanderings,
a lotus lifting from earth
ascending from the center.

Instead her cheeks
stung by brambles,
eyes closed, branches
snapping back as she follows,
always in your wake.

There is an apparent definition
fundamentally

unbelievable, called: belief—set it aside
don't suspend the senses   (belief)   or

photographs made
in total darkness

taken away from real events but still referring
I am losing . . . the light alert, crested then crestfallen

NOTE [HADES TO PERSEPHONE]

Along the periphery she strains at the limits.

One more and you will never still.

The answer is the length of my body
by the cast of the sea

danger not invented but
visited, situated—

I lined them up and ate them all

      Death

is not the opposite

nor the same as sleep
an opening, peephole:

The cloak falls——his

(epistle, missive, prism of, between
I see: I live to see, and even
the woven pouch at my thigh
with morsels of the world above
he severs; the pleasure of crushed
mint or bitter nettles clinging,
captive, devours,   I)

candor

I dare not describe

I have heard the real world shivers and splinters
but do not believe it.

The wind is touched with their scent,
those who speak at all.

The new dead arrive thin and frozen
but I will not frighten.

My king is no farmer to be ruined by famine,
no shepherd following a woolly flock.

He depends on nothing.
I will make myself worthy.

LETTER [DEMETER TO PERSEPHONE]

Am I the only one to notice the soft layer of haze above snow?

You say you see butterflies in the skeleton pelvis, well,
what about the larger hand of the clock?
Or a cauldron for boiling water?

Did you, do you ever stop falling?

                                 I repeat your name
                                     a word

                                 it almost means
                                   nothing

Do you remember encyclopedias?
I piled up the books so you could reach the table.

Now the only way to recall you is the shape
of your walking away.

Only a mother could manufacture such a story:
the earth opened and pulled her down.

She shows my picture all over town
and worries the details of my molestation.

Terrified she screamed for mother . . .
but I did not scream.

She says it is like having an arm ripped
from her body. But think, Mother,

what it is to be an arm ripped from a body.
Bloody shoulder bulb, fingers twitching, useless.

Did she expect me to starve?
To wither away, mourning the tulip, primrose, crocus?

And if I have changed, so be it.
He did not choose me for my slim ankles or silken tresses.

She moans and tears her hair   *Unfair!*
There was so much I longed to teach her.

Sad Mother, who thinks she knows so much—
teach the farmer to grow seed.

The fields await instruction.

In him is a loneliness so complete he cannot feel it.
I grow to fit it.

     My hips, under his, give way.

Everywhere the air is thin with ghosts—they float
like mist across the edges of the eye, gone

when the head turns to acknowledge. Their courtesy
makes a path for me to pass, a cleaner atmosphere.

We are not just lovers,
but no one understands this.

My mother lies with Poseidon, Dionysus, Helios, Hermes
and is unchanged. I am

becoming something
other than I was.

     A consort. A Queen.

No more a maiden but still with maiden hands.
It's true that I am less without him

but when he sees me

all the gold of this world glows against the marble walls
and the veins of the deep stones blush with color.

His bones make a soft place for me on his granite bed.
His touch is the sweet glance of the past, but his laugh—

he has always been expecting me.

Even his hunger

even death, his craving

so lovely he says

be wary he says

ice and a woman in impractical clothing reach for me

she means nothing to me . . .

but we know it is impossible like a dark morning for very long

Refuse to stay.

Or one day *c* might be the first letter.

> *chercher* (to search)
> *perdu* (lost)
> *oublier* (to forget)

Chasm; to join together in chasm.

Now, the earth
is cold

Celsius

(you cannot stay)

Once you took small steps,
        determined to remain upright.

                An elephant-on-wheels taught you to walk.

            Do you still name the animals?

Here all the swans are made of ice.
Is death like melting?

LETTER [PERSEPHONE TO DEMETER]

When I met him I forgot the days when green
came in from the fields and stayed for dinner. Sundays into
        long days into drawn out sunsets and desired delectables,
over-spilling with tabulation. Here is a tabula fuchsia of disasters and
        symphonies lasting—

Mother, nothing but spindles holds us together. Whether
        by might or lightning the dragon-daylilies platooned
into desire, fired and returned. Now I rise over the horizon, higher and
        higher, see me? "there!" (missed) "there!" (gone) "there!"
Coincidence or winter uprooted whatever vascular implements
        I once possessed. Catapulted me out of contentment. Out of
green and verve, my virtual slumber. Now,

        like the deaf sight-reading rhyme, I am a thin
slip of sound, light residue of moon on the night.

Dozens of cattle lowing in the overturned cattle cars
cow bodies crushed together in sub-zero—

a terrific glare on the terrible roads.

Stave. Solstice.

The shape of you walking away is not an angel.

Wither. Dispatch.

The shape of you fallen, arms out . . .

This grief has waves and is cold and will not be described
with other words.

Hurry mutter the hungry.
Come home before it freezes.

I watched men come and go.
Once I saw one leave on crutches.

War or polio
(usually a mother will supply the details).

But she never told me how to be a woman.
I never knew why some men walked and others stumbled.

Once mistress of a fabulous garden: bamboo
along the old stone walls, a dogwood, Japanese maple,

and myrtle dotted with wild strawberries.
She told me

> *for a woman, sex is like a house—men*
> *muddy the furniture.*

But she is wrong. Here, I am more than a guest.

I eat what I am offered.

My king and I welcome the dead she sends us.

to find you gone

is more than I
can bear

bird

up out of
mortuary, aviary

I hold
your memories
first words
favorite animals

nostos (return home)
neistha (return)
nesan (survive)
nasate (she approaches)

without me
the path will not

endure the present
landmarks or forced
scenery
homesick, you circle
you will not find
or journey or
bear children

Dressed as Hermes, Adonis visits and says
he brings letters from Pandora, Echo, Psyche.

He places a golden box before me.
On the lock my name is spelled in rubies.
When I open it, the stones
scatter and the settings vanish.
I gather the gems and for safe keeping
place them beneath my tongue.
Inside a humming from under a veil
of warm wax. My fingers soften
as I remove the outer layer:

minikin, frozen bodies of hundreds of children.
When I scream, I swallow my teeth by mistake.
Rubies but no sounds spill from my mouth.

This world will certainly be displaced,
the cold has grown too great.

The boatman hurries to loosen his rope—
he crosses the nets.

It keeps raining.

When I said your eyes lit up
I meant they pushed the gold out
through the green.

But see how empty the light is,
whereas the wave (so many colors)
coming through and through.

The rain, a tensile adhesive,
holding and holding me—

I slip through: the nets, the residue,
I must slip through.

[TWO]

There is no life higher than the grasstops
Or the hearts of sheep, and the wind
Pours by like destiny, bending
Everything in one direction.
I can feel it trying
To funnel my heat away.
If I pay the roots of the heather
Too close attention, they will invite me
To whiten my bones among them.

SYLVIA PLATH

I walk the streets, pick up speech,
lose my way—one world, another.

Words like "whore" or "bench" or "cap" are what I find,
all that's left by others.

Consigned to lifetime night-sweeps, I curse
the conservation of the paltry

but sweep it up, this rot. And knowing not
with what to hold it, build a pantry.

A fleet of jars: seedless jam, okra, three-corn relish.
Sterilized, preserved in brine, from seed, from soil, my despair.

The thready, fetal pods. Crisp and bitter teeth. My sweet,
deep blood. I walk the streets.

Days passed and shone until, innocent with questions,
I asked *this? this is but a refuse of packed-up light.*
Wilting, I wander, mocked by helpless angels
whose foreheads belie a city of dreary projections:
a junkyard topsoil of roots and sidewalks,
bulldozed bodies of badly pruned trees.
A pasture is something a lonely lot dreams of.
And I am a post, pinned to this street, like the memory
of a view of trees. Cling to me bird—rest on the small sign
that is my only arm. Park is to nestle as sad is sad.
Letter for letter the writ was written, a radical shifting
in the part and spare parts world of concrete places.
Where is the old refusal? Grass in place of names.
Once, even the trees were hungry. Sleeping
is something I do to forget the inching and inching
of the onward city.

The sixth side of the room
is a quick blue ceiling, lighter than fog.

Outside a squirrel stretches out, unhindered by branches.
The room folds but does not collapse.

Flying has always been a matter of color.
A plain brown portfolio, from the outside: plain and brown.

A plain brown pinafore, from the inside: *piano forte.*
I go out into it, while the trees are still slicked with ice.

While the words are *am*, *is*, *my, daughter.*
A path of bony trees and broken deer.

The sky does not exist, of course, just a certain lightness about the head—
windows no one has ever looked out of:

Spring is not so very promising as it is the thing
that looking back was fire, promising:
ignition, aspiration; it was not under my thumb.

Now when I pretend a future it is the moment
he holds the thing I say new-born,
delicate, sure to begin moving but

I am burned out of it like the melody underneath
(still not under my thumb)—
was he ambiguous, amphibian?

Underneath, his voice, the many ways
he gathers oxygen; it will not stop raining
until the buds push through the brittle trees.

If they fail we will not survive,
washed and washed with rain, will we?
No, we are not there yet.

She is pushing me two ways until
I am inside the paradox, the many lungs,
and they're at it again, gathering oxygen;

no wonder I am wrung out
holding out for the promise of
something secret, after—

I no longer love you.
I don't think I do.
Although once I was sure
I never loved you before.

But now I know—since
I no longer love you
(writing) "I no longer do"—
that I did (once) love you.

And if later, sometime,
I come to know
I no longer love you,
then today, now, I do.

Say weather is not what it is
and do not go out.
If you have a window to watch with
watch. If not wait.

Wait. It is likely
you will not go out.
As always, you are always
inside the city.

Even when you are outside,
you are inside the city.
A precise point on the map:
here and here and here

and everywhere there is
a mountain
that is a big wall
that is the city.

But landmarks are mutable,
you are removable; something
will block out these traces
of available light. Once I

believed in weather
and tried to plan accordingly.
Now there is: the window,
the forecast, last platform.

The day is too bright.

Everyone has already seen it or one just like it,
their necks like poles or bent accordions

and all around me poisonous berries on beautiful trees
not worth describing.

No one eats anymore.
No one makes mistakes.

A city grows up to house millions;
cherished fields destroyed willingly.

The surface is carved over and over in names.

Some call it love, some obligation—
though neither true, we pile up and prosper.

Won, like a trinket, I obey and am nothing.
Hear?—she calls me:

from other rooms, across deep rivers,
complains I'm never where she left me.

She forbids me meadows, untilled prairies for fear
I'll find the flower whose hundred stems grow from one root.

So I keep to the craggy enclaves, outside watchfulness:
mountains, shores, places which sustain no vegetation—

UNSENT LETTER [PERSEPHONE TO HADES]

I was a fool not to suspect—
but lived long among the dead.

Remember how our nights numbered and mingled?

Now feel it quicken: the end of maidenhood.

I paid my season and stayed where she could see me.

But I'm not like the girl she meant to rescue
and she has not my mother's voice
scratched through from crying.

She does not see my gravid walk or swollen wrists.

Here is a hollow that ripens and fulls,
a thick mist estuary
but solid, temporal—

it is time I go where no one bargains.

LETTER [HADES TO PERSEPHONE]

Soon there will be no room even for wind.
Half-decomposed petals swirling
over the nubile pine-tree line.
I whisper these words to you at bedtime,
come home, stay in my procession
even if the future holds more crinoline hedges.

Before I leave I will turn some of these young girls
to birds. So they might fly.

Human eyes will guide them,
bird bodies carry them.

Their singing will torture the gods.

I never cared much for flowers,
servants to bees and beauty.

Tell the daughters to go down through darkness:
there they will find me.

And though we may bring death back with us,
every year we will return alive.

The storm was a new widow
letting her veil down over the mountains
a blue-black caress

wiping away our footsteps
making the sand rise like steam over the dunes.
On the way down we stopped together.

In the tree-skeleton cemetery
the trees stripped clean, gold-burnished
by fire and floods. She told me marriage

is something you live through
or maybe I told her. She told me
the clouds would cushion the jagged mountains

when they fall. She told me she would
break the net to save the world,
to make my footsteps green.

Do you have a spare self or shadow to keep me cool
take off this dreadful skin of future pressing in
the present humid, slippery?

If only I could photograph myself out of this
be a man writing about animals or history

extinct fauna, husked mollusks . . .
but I can't.

Look how the months swing by and taunt me—

a viscous oyster waiting for nacre
to coat my unseens, despair polishing,
bending light through me.

I will sell my long hair for two mother-of-pearl buttons,
unclasp my heart from its open bird cage

but not put desire away.
Remember, when you see me, I am inside who I was.

ABOUT THE AUTHOR

Rachel Zucker grew up in Greenwich Village and was educated at Yale University and the Iowa Writer's Workshop. Her poems have appeared in various journals, including Barrow Street, Pleiades, *and* The American Poetry Review, *as well as in the anthology* Best American Poetry. *She lives in New York City with her husband, Joshua Goren, and their two sons.*